What Times Are

Jacques Rancière

What Times Are We Living In?

A Conversation with Eric Hazan

Translated by Steven Corcoran

polity

Originally published in French as *En quel temps vivons-nous ? Conversation avec Eric Hazan* © La Fabrique Éditions, 2017

This English edition © 2021 by Polity Press

Polity Press
65 Bridge Street
Cambridge CB2 1UR, UK

Polity Press
101 Station Landing
Suite 300
Medford, MA 02155, USA

ISBN-13: 978-1-5095-3698-6
ISBN-13: 978-1-5095-3699-3 (paperback)

A catalogue record for this book is available from the British Library.

Typeset in 12.5 on 15 pt Adobe Garamond by
Servis Filmsetting Ltd, Stockport, Cheshire
Printed and bound in the UK by CPI Group (UK) Ltd, Croydon

The publisher has used its best endeavours to ensure that the URLs for external websites referred to in this book are correct and active at the time of going to press. However, the publisher has no responsibility for the websites and can make no guarantee that a site will remain live or that the content is or will remain appropriate.

Every effort has been made to trace all copyright holders, but if any have been overlooked the publisher will be pleased to include any necessary credits in any subsequent reprint or edition.

For further information on Polity, visit our website: politybooks.com

This book took the form of a 'conversation' after a compromise was reached. At La Fabrique we wanted Rancière to express his thoughts on the times we are living in, but he himself didn't feel the need to do so. Then, perhaps worn down by my asking, he told me one day that, if I presented him with some questions, he would reply to them. The task seemed to me a difficult one, although the aim was clear: to get Rancière to elaborate on things he had recently put forward in articles and interviews – on novelty in 'our times' and on what in them is continuous with the past, on the link between representation and democracy, on the end of work as the form of a common world to come, on hopes for a community of struggle that is also a community of life, on the new caution that we must adopt when speaking about such apparently simple notions as 'people', 'insurrection' or 'history' . . . But what questions should be asked and where to start?

I took some months to decide, then ended up by setting down one piece of the puzzle and, Rancière playing the game, the rest fell nicely into place. The conversation unfolded in written form, at a lively pace, between August 2016 and February 2017. The reader will be the judge of whether the result lives up to the question posed in the title of this short book.

E.H.

ERIC HAZAN In *Hatred of Democracy*, published in France in 2005, you put forward some rules designed to permit a representative system to declare itself democratic: short and non-renewable electoral mandates, a monopoly of the people's representatives over the drafting of laws, control against the interference of economic powers in electoral processes ... In other texts from the same period, you suggest that a large role be given to drawing lots in the selection of a 'government staff', to prevent its being composed of those who 'like power' and are adept at taking it.

It is now more than twelve years since *Hatred* was written. Do you think that democracy is the central notion around which political questions continue to revolve? That the choice of those who represent us remains determinant? Have we not seen the growing decay of the representative system of government in recent years? Is the question today not to find a way to get rid of it – and at last to live without government?

JACQUES RANCIÈRE *Hatred of Democracy* laid out a reflection on the idea of democracy, not a political agenda. The reflection set out from a contradiction that saw, in states that defined themselves as *democracies*, fierce campaigns develop denouncing *democracy* as the reign of mass individualism and the destruction of the social link. The book's central thesis was that democracy is not a political regime, that it is the egalitarian condition, the anarchic condition of the very existence of a specifically political power – but also, by the same token, the condition that the exercise of power strives incessantly to repress. I showed that what we commonly call politics is actually the contradiction in act that brings the exercise of power to rest on the democratic principle that contradicts it and of which it is the contradiction. This is the framework within which I studied the opposition of principle between democratic logic and representative logic and the forms of crossover between them. I recalled in particular a certain number of principles and rules that can be deduced from the democratic principle and that are liable to inject more democracy into institutions, for example drawing lots and short, non-renewable and non-cumulative mandates. I recalled these rules and principles not as recipes to apply for 'revitalizing democracy', as they say today, but as demands suited to creating a break with the prevailing view, which assimilates democracy and representation, and to showing that our representative regimes are in fact increasingly oligarchic and that, in France, republican campaigns against the horrors of equality are the theoretical crowning of the process of growing inequality in our societies and our institutions.[1]

I admit to finding comical the idea that we have moved beyond all that. The republican campaign that I denounced back then has intensified ever since, becoming the main national cause – which, for example, makes the wearing of this or that swimming costume 'the question' on which the future of our civilization depends. As for the decay of the representative system, this is

---

1 I take advantage of this occasion to point out that the regularly announced work by Jacques Rancière titled *How to Revitalise Democracy* does not exist.

an outdated notion that has sustained the hopes and illusions of a 'radical' left since the 1880s, a left always given to seeing in the low participation rates in this election or that the proof that there has been massive disinvestment from the electoral system. But there is no decay of the representative system. Institutions are not living beings: they do not die from their illnesses. This system is staying the course and finds ways to accommodate the anomalies and monsters that it secretes. Through its very mechanisms, it creates a place for those who claim to represent the unrepresented, and it turns its own mediocrity into a principle of resignation to its necessity. Facing this, recent extra- or anti-parliamentary movements have not created any real alternative political space. The squares movements, which have produced the most vigorous affirmations of democracy in recent years, have been unable to lead to the creation of political movements autonomous of state agendas. Their heritage has sometimes dissipated, sometimes extended into alternative forms, but it has also been captured by 'left of the left' parties such as Podemos or Syriza, which play the game of electoral programmes and of alliances and negotiations between gov-

4

ernmental parties. The energy of Occupy Wall Street gave impetus to the Bernie Sanders campaign, which in the end was left no choice but to support Hillary Clinton. And, in France, the electoral circumstances risk being marked by the usual stampede of leftist souls who subscribe to a logic of the 'least worst'. Those who once asked us to vote for Hollande because he wasn't as bad as Sarkozy will urge us this time to vote for Macron because he isn't as bad as Fillon, or for Fillon because he isn't as bad as Marine Le Pen, and in five years' time to support Marine Le Pen because she isn't as bad as her niece. The brains of Nuit debout [Up All Night] called upon us to say: we will never vote socialist again. I think that he should rather have said: we want no more presidents or presidential elections. I think that a head-on campaign challenging the 'democratic' primaries and the very procedure of the presidential election was a wholly logical outcome of the movement and precisely the occasion to mark the fact that democracy is something other than the choosing of the few by the many.

Living without government is certainly a great aim to have. But this was similarly the case in 2005, and indeed in 1850, when the defeated revolutionaries seized on the idea of 'direct leg-islation by the people' and began to oppose the 'association' or the 'social' to the government. This means that we are no closer to reaching this goal than we were in 1850. To get closer to reach-ing it, we must begin precisely by shedding the idea that this goal is carried by the general run of things. We must do away with the old Marxist idea that the world of domination secretes its own destruction, that 'all that is solid melts into air', and that the institutions and beliefs that sus-tained the old order will dissolve by themselves in the famous 'icy waters of egotistical calcula-tion'. According to this logic, states, parliaments, religions and ideologies will supposedly disap-pear through capitalism's very development. Still today, the dominant discourse on 'neolib-eralism' sees in neoliberalism the moment when economic domination is laid bare through the dissolution of all beliefs and institutions. But the fact is that we have ever more states – even supra-states – and ever more government; that the representative system does not cease to gain in strength by following its natural, anti-democratic bent; that 'liberal' capitalism does not cease to impose ever new norms and regulations; that religion today plays the massive role that it does; and that nationalisms and ethnicisms, along with all reactionary ideologies, have been powerfully reinforced in recent decades.

I certainly understand that the dominant state of the world is one thing and that our thinking is not constrained to fall into line with it – on the contrary, it is sustained by the energies of those who fight against it. Yet these energies themselves must not feed on fabricated analyses and sophisms regarding this state of affairs. In particular, they must overcome the reasoning that transforms the brutal advances of state and capitalist oligarchies into signs that these oligarchies are increasingly exposed and rendered powerless, and that sees in the defeats of democracy the tumbling of the illusions, paving the way to the final struggle. Defeats of democracy are defeats of equality, not the flight of illusions. More profoundly, we must get out of the logic that enlists historical developments in the service of one's desires by interpreting the history of domination as that of a world of appearances destined to crumble for the benefit of naked reality. 'Appearances' are solid. Hence also the necessity to leave behind the pseudo-radical logic according to which the battle for institutions and the procedures of politics (which is not that of choosing representatives) are disqualified as mere appearances and all political equality is returned to a simple inverted reflection or deceptive instrument of capital's domination. When it comes to radicality, this logic strictly shares the official view of things: just like this view, it bases itself on the presupposition that the representative system is the simple expression of an underlying social reality. The official version casts this system as an expression of the opinions of a people deemed to exist before this system. The critical version casts this system as the mystified expression of a class struggle that also exists before this system. But the people is not the great collective body expressed in representation. It is the quasi-body produced by the functioning of this system. And representation is not an expression, or even an instrument, of class struggle. It is a form of this struggle's existence: not the passive expression of a pre-given reality but an effective matrix for constructing the common, for producing significations, behaviours and affects. The way in which our electoral system creates the body and the emotions of a 'true people from below' is a significant example of this today.

The modern metapolitical view turns politics into the expression of a socioeconomic process situated 'underneath' or 'behind'.[2] But appearances and reality are not what there is. What there is is different forms of construction and symbolization of the common, which are all equally real and equally traversed by the conflict between equality and inequality. Constructing different forms of life also amounts to constructing different views of the 'problems' with which the dominant order presents us. In no way do I believe that inequality would disappear, as though by enchantment, if one decided to have assemblies drawn by lot. The question is, indeed, to know, first of all, who this 'one' is. I set out simply from the fact that this idea, which is perfectly logical, is completely at odds with the system now in existence and that it defines a view of politics that can be usefully incorporated into an alternative vision of the world and implemented in a political practice that avoids the choice between getting integrated into the representative system

2 On the notion of metapolitics as the return of politics to an underlying reality, see chapter 4 of my *Disagreement: Philosophy and Politics*, trans. Julie Rose (Minnesota: University of Minnesota Press, 2004 [1995]).

or simply denouncing this system's illusion to the advantage of 'real' struggles.

ERIC HAZAN   Aren't the examples you give precisely symptoms of the *withering*, of the *last throes* of the representative system, which you describe as 'staying the course'? In Greece, for example, in summer 2015, the fact that a government massively buoyed up by a series of elections took decisions contrary to its commitments and to a clearly expressed popular will – does this not go to confirm what the then German finance minister, Wolfgang Schäuble, said at the time, 'we cannot allow elections to change anything whatsoever'? In the same register of ideas, does the presidential election that's brewing in France not appear as a masquerade to a large part of the population? Isn't there something entirely novel here, in the fifty years in which this election has been in existence and raising hopes?[3]

3 [Translator's note: The French presidential election is a two-round election. If no candidate wins an absolute majority in the first round, a run-off is held two weeks later between the two candidates who received the most votes. Since the Fifth Republic was established in 1958, there have been eleven presidential elections. The 2017 presidential election was held on 23 April and 7 May 2017. With no candidate securing an absolute majority

JACQUES RANCIÈRE   If the representative system were in its death throes each time a left-wing party betrayed its electoral promises, it would actually have been dead for a good century, which is not the case. The objection rests on a false idea, which equates three different things with one another – representation, election and democracy – and takes the representative system to result in the simple 'democratic' illusion whereby people are subjected to a power whose source they imagine themselves to be. In this case, it can be logically deduced that a politician who declares that the people cannot be left to decide anything what-soever is thus admitting the lie of representation and destroying the belief that had established mass adherence to the system. But such is not the case for several reasons.

First – and I've recalled this point several times – representation, as a principle, is not democracy. Democracy is not the choosing of representatives; it is the power of those who are not qualified to exercise power. The prevailing doxa depicts

in the first round, the run-off was held between the top two, Emmanuel Macron of En Marche! and Marine Le Pen of the National Front (FN), and the former won by a decisive margin.]

representation as a movement that sets out from below: the people exists as a collective body and chooses for itself some representatives. But a political people is not a pre-existent given; it is a result. It is not the people who are represented but representation that produces a certain type of people. And representation, in the thinking of those who invented the representative system, means that there is a part of society that is naturally apt, thanks to its position, to represent the general interests of the society. In the vision of the American founding fathers, the class of enlightened landowners represented that privileged part. At home in France we saw, with the murderous assemblies of 1848 and 1871, just what this 'enlightened' class was. Thereafter, the logic of the system turned autonomous: representation has become a job undertaken by a class of professional politicians that, for the main part, is self-reproducing and has this self-reproduction validated by the specific form of people it produces, namely the electoral body. The electoral body reconfirms the power of this class by choosing from among its fractions. If, independently of the electoral system, there are no autonomous and robust democratic powers that construct another people – an egalitarian people in movement – then the hierarchical logic of reproducing 'legitimate' representatives (that is, the caste of professionals of power) will prevail. Nowadays this science of reproducing governmental oligarchies has come to identify itself with knowledge about the common production of wealth, in other words with the prevailing economic science. This is the framework in which a German finance minister would recall that the rational decisions upon which European prosperity depends cannot be subject to the vicissitudes of the Greek electorate. But in so doing he did not need to contradict electoral arithmetic by announcing the privilege of the few over the many. For, in the European framework, the Greek electors are the ones who play the role of the minority that has no right to impose its will on the majority. Schaüble's view on this matter was by no means opposed to that of his own electorate.

This is the first point about the representative system. The second concerns the modes of adherence to this system. The received wisdom is that the system works on condition that the electors believe that they decide who represents them and what are the policies that these representatives have to carry out. This way of conceiving is very simplistic. In fact belief does not found adherence; rather adherence founds belief. Belief is the subjective effect of an order of things, the way in which this order is internalized. The French presidential system is sustained less through the hopes it raises than through the discouragement it produces. Now, this discouragement affects those who don't vote as much as it does those who do. It impacts hopes for revolutionary pathways as much as hopes for improvement through electoral means. Inegalitarian logic, furthermore, provides those whom it renders inferior with the means to believe that in this way they exercise their superiority. One consents not because one is a dupe, but in order to show that one is not a dupe. This is what I called, following Jacotot, the logic of superior inferiors: you submit to a form of domination to the extent that it gives you the possibility to show contempt for it. Most forms of domination today function in this way: there is no need to 'believe' in media messages, to be seduced by publicity images or to hope for something from the people one elects. The system works very well through unbelief, which is tantamount to saying that this supposed disbelief is the normal mode of belief today. Of course 'disbelief' is an overly general word, which covers subjective affects and dispositions of diverse types. It would be necessary to go in depth into the diverse modes of subjectivation that it covers. But key here is doing away with the idea of domination as a great coherent system, an organic totality that logically produces the institutions and subjective attitudes that correspond to its needs. The state of affairs through which domination works is a combination of heterogenous elements and arrangements. The ways of adhering to it or distancing oneself from it are themselves heterogeneous combinations of affects and forms of consciousness in relation to which the themes of disenchantment and disinvestment are ineffective simplifications.

ERIC HAZAN Wasn't the movement that emerged in the spring of 2016,[4] with all its

4 [Translator's note: The movement in the spring of 2016 arose from protests against a set of proposed labour reforms known as *loi Travail* (labour law) or the El Khomri law, named after Myriam El Khomri, the labour minister who promulgated these reforms. He served as labour minister of the Valls government from 2 September 2015 to 10 May 2017. The law came into force on 9 August 2016. The movement broadly organized around the slogan Against the Labour Law and the Its World. As

weaknesses and contradictions, nonetheless an advance on . . . 1850? Did it not mark the end of the illusion that you denounce, 'the old Marxist idea that the world of domination secretes its own destruction'? In its disqualification of traditional politics, it seems to me that it did not attack appearances but indeed sought to construct the 'different views' you seek. In short, are we not witnessing a major subjective shift in the ways of fighting against the existing order?

JACQUES RANCIÈRE   This advance is by no means certain. In 1850 it was easy for militant workers to oppose the association or 'the social' to a capitalist power and to a state power conceived of as parasitic. What appeared at that moment, notably through the development of an entire network of worker associations, was the idea that work constitutes a common world, the immense horizontal structure of a system of production and exchange

Rancière mentions in the interview, the movement quickly saw the labour law as a specific manifestation of a world of inequality that needs to be challenged and changed. The slogan Against the Labour Law and Its World was thus intended as a synthesis not only of the stakes of this mobilization but also of the broader historical conjuncture.]

that can function by itself and without hierarchy. The development of various socialisms, such as that of anarcho-syndicalism, was sustained precisely by this vision of a future in which relations mediated by the abstractions of money and the commodity would (again) become direct relations between producers. This evidence of work as a common world already there, a world ready to take back what had been alienated in commodity relations and in state structures, has disappeared from the contemporary universe of financial capitalism, delocalized industry and the extension of the precariat – also a universe in which capitalist and statist mediation is everywhere. And, essentially, the famous *loi Travail* was a declaration about the definitive expiry of work as a common world. Some respond to this with sabre-rattling about the end of illusions of work and of labour value. Others see in it the sign that what is henceforth required by post-Fordist capitalism is life in full and no longer labour power; and from this they deduce the emergence of a new 'biopolitical' movement, a movement of life itself following on from the classic worker movement. But the protesters of the spring of 2016 spontaneously perceived something else: the official declaration that henceforth work no longer has any reason to forge community relations in our advanced societies, that it ought to be merely how each individual manages their 'human capital'. Another manner of stating this has been the judicial repression, by now systematic, of forms of worker struggle hitherto considered to be part and parcel of the risks of social conflicts (sentences handed out to Goodyear workers and to protesters against Air France). The unprecedented alliance between unionized workers and the unorganized collectives of Nuit debout[5] was also significant from this point of view, for whoever remembers the ferocity of clashes between leftists and unionists in days gone by.

But this also means that this movement, considerable as it was, cannot be situated on any simple evolutionary timeline. It at once attested and masked the fact that, if work continues to be

5 [Translator's note: The assemblies of Nuit debout were an especially visible part of this movement of 2016, coming as it did after five years of events across the world that involved movements of occupying public squares: the Spanish Indignados, Gezi in Istanbul, Tahrir in Cairo, Occupy Wall Street, and so on. As elsewhere, Nuit debout was a matter of occupying a public square in which diverse social strata, generations and political sensibilities were brought together around a common goal.]

a stake of struggle and a principle of community, it no longer forms a world. Work is no longer the always-already-there form of a world to come, which it still was in 1968, even if the symbolic function that the working class was attributed in left-wing thought conflicted with the 'reality' that its 'legitimate' representatives sought to manage. Further, though, it has not really been replaced in that function. The current favour for a universal basic income (UBI) testifies to this in its way. UBI began as the expression of a new militancy borne by historical developments, the militancy of cognitive workers in the post-Fordist era. This 'historical' movement has remained purely hypothetical. What has taken place in its stead is the interim of movements of occupation. UBI has since been floated as a state measure aimed at compensating for deindustrialization. There is no longer any community already there that guarantees the community to come. The community has become above all an object of desire. This is the prominent phenomenon to have emerged from the movement of squares and occupations. On the one hand, it is indeed true that the movement in the spring of 2016 produced a break with the operation of what in France is understood by politics. We should recall that the Spanish movement of 15 May and those that followed it had almost no resonance in France, because the major issue here at the time was the great socialist democratic primary. From this point of view the movement in the spring of 2016 certainly gave rise to a break, the affirmation of a people different from that of the electoral process. But it was more a matter of making up ground than one of taking any significant step forward in thought and action. Additionally, what has been noted – again, more strongly in the French case than in the aforementioned movements – is the extent to which this other people is more an object of desire than a form in movement. One knows how to give a figure to the requirement of this other people, but does not know which organs and which forms to give to its constitution. The role allotted to the assembly as a figure of the equal people in which each person speaks about whatever they like for an equal amount of time gives eloquent testimony to this. Testifying to this in another way is the burgeoning of themes such as 'destituent' power, taken from Giorgio Agamben, or 'exodus', as extolled by Paolo Virno. On the one hand, the affirmed break is deprived of any symbolic and lived world to lean on. On the other, it has difficulty finding forms through which to develop itself. This is why the idea that the system is moribund and ready to collapse remains convenient. It fills in the gap between the current breaks and the hoped-for future and allows one to imagine, alternatively, that, by giving the system a little nudge with the elbow, one will make it come crashing down, or that by pulling out of it one will make it dissolve. In the booklet *Premières mesures révolutionnaires* [*First Revolutionary Measures*], published by La Fabrique three years ago, I read this: 'the decrepit state of democratic capitalism is such that its collapse will be on an international scale regardless of where the first trembling is situated'.[6] I am not at all sure that this sort of illusion vanished last spring.

ERIC HAZAN   One remark, or rather a parenthesis: at the beginning of *Premières mesures révolutionnaires*, there is a clearly stated postulate according to which the insurrection took place

---

6 Eric Hazan and Kamo, *Premières mesures révolutionnaires*, La Fabrique, 2013, p. 15.

and was victorious. The book deals with what one might do afterwards – and not with the chances of any such insurrection arising, or with its conditions of success. It thus does not involve any illusion. The sentence that you cite is clearly a reference to the international explosion that followed the events of the spring of 1848 and the spring of 1968 in France.

That said, the discouragement you mention, and on which the French presidential system feeds, impacts, you say, revolutionary hopes as much as hopes for improvement through the electoral path. Isn't that talking down the novelty of the movement that took place last spring? Can one speak about discouragement, when demonstrations were held right throughout France and, at the head of their marches, school and university students gathered together with unorganized youths and workers, in small groups that bore the flags of their unions? The media was careful not to mention that in the demonstration on 15 September the *cortège de tête*[7] represented a good

7 [Translator's note: The expression *cortège de tête*, which designates the leading contingent in a march, has recently come to take on a precise meaning in extra-parliamentary politics in France. Occupying the head of the march has traditionally been

half of all participants. Of course, this youth in revolt was only a small minority by comparison to the millions of electors, but ought we really to count in this way?

JACQUES RANCIÈRE That a system produces an effect of discouragement does not mean that everyone is discouraged. There are even many electors who keep their chins up. My remarks were not aimed at giving a negative diagnosis of the movement in the spring of 2016. They aimed to call into question the logic on which the large number of analyses rest, and I would call it the logic of communicating vessels: the idea that a reduction in hope in the representative system produces an increase in the energies disposed towards alternatives to this system. In the last

a role reserved to trade unions and political organizations keen to set the tone, but during the movement against the *loi Travail* this space was significantly taken by a diverse mix of unorganized youths, rank-and-file union members, public servants, researchers, unemployed persons and so on, while organized political formations were taking up the rear. As Eric Hazan is keen to underline, the unorganized aspect of this leading 'contingent' of the demonstrations during the movement in the spring of 2016, whose diversity of composition distinguishes it from a simple identification with black-bloc tactics, represented a novel approach to political protest on the French scene.]

instance, this logic always rests on the belief that the shedding of illusion (the electoral system) produces a rise in the power of the true (the social movement, true struggles, etc.). Things have never worked this way. The logics that get bodies and minds moving are in fact much more complex intersections of heterogeneous logics, as is shown by the fact that extra-parliamentary movements were at their peak in times when the parliamentary system still fed hopes. Today, conversely, electoral despondency readily finds its counterpart in half-resigned movements of protest and 'radical' revolutionary theories that often borrow their arguments and their tone from the disenchanted theories of civilizational catastrophe.

It can be said that the spring of 2016 moved us on from this despondency. There is no doubt that youths mobilized throughout the whole of France, and there can be no comparison between their number and the number of electors. On the other hand, it is not wrong to compare their number with those of other segments of the youth population: the youth of the 'creative class', who moves with dynamic ease around the so-called neoliberal order; the youth who mobilizes for the Front national and for the Manifs pour tous [Demos for All];[8] the youth who heeds calls for the war of religion; and the great mass of those so-called youths of the banlieues, who were indifferent or even hostile to the demonstrations that took place last spring. One needs to be more precise when invoking the 'novelty' of this latter movement. There is always some novelty when one goes from resignation to protest. But this novelty is itself caught in a logic where the first stake is to resist the enemy's offensives – a resistance that, from a strictly pragmatic viewpoint, proved unable to force a retreat on this occasion, unlike what happened with the proposed pension reforms in 1995[9] and with the bill

8 [Translator's note: The Manifs pour tous took place in cities throughout France, essentially in 2013 and 2014, and were organized to oppose gay marriage, before broadening out into a defence of the family. They are significant for being the largest right-wing mobilization since the 1930s; they included a number of right-wing groups, such as Génération identitaire, together with many traditional Catholic and Protestant as well as Muslim and Jewish groups.]

9 [Translator's note: In 1995 a massive strike movement and waves of demonstrations erupted against a set of proposed reforms to welfare, known as the Juppé plan, after Prime Minister Alain Juppé. After weeks of mass strikes and demonstrations, which drew broad popular support, the government formally renounced the plan.]

to institute the CPE[10] in 2006. We should, of course, separate the accountancy of objective gains from a movement's increases in subjective power. Indeed the phenomenon of Nuit debout was important from this point of view, that is, for the transformation of a resistance movement into the movement of a self-affirming community taking possession of its own time and space. But, by entering, rather more meekly than happened elsewhere, into the dynamic of the movement of squares and occupations, it essentially took up its forms and encountered the same problems. On Place de la République, as in Liberty Plaza or the Puerta del Sol, the centrality of the assembly form at once displayed the power of a desire for

10 [Translator's note: the *contrat de premier ébauche* (CPE: first employment contract) was a new form of employment contract, pushed in spring 2006 in France by Prime Minister Dominique de Villepin. This employment contract, available solely to employees under 26, would have made it easier for the employer to fire employees by removing the need to provide reasons for dismissal for an initial 'trial period' of two years, in exchange for some financial guarantees for employees, the intention being to make employers less reluctant to hire additional staff. However, establishing the CPE required amending the Equality of Opportunity Act (*loi sur l'égalité des chances*), and this made it so unpopular that soon massive protests were held, mostly by young students, and the government rescinded the amendment.]

community and equality and showed how this desire inhibits itself and shuts itself within its own image – within the staging of the happiness of being together. The problem, however, is not to go from individualism to community but from one form of community to another.

The spring of 2016, again, made palpably current the idea of a community of struggle that is also a community of life. It simultaneously restaged the problem of the liaison between them, between the process of constitution of an autonomous people and that of the constitution of a fighting force against the enemy. All modern history is traversed by the tension between class struggle, conceived of as the formation of an army to defeat the enemy, and class struggle, grasped as a people in secession through the invention of its own autonomous institutions and forms of life. This tension found some resolution so long as one and the same people could figure both as the army of workers in combat and that of emancipated producers. It explodes, however, when it is no longer the factories, or even the universities, that are being occupied, or the premises of social services that enable a presence to be given to the forces in conflict, but instead the vacant space of city squares in which the community symbolizes itself as an assembly in times of egalitarian speech, while slogans such as 'everyone hates the police' resound in the adjacent streets, where the destruction of a few ATMs serves as derisory compensation for the destruction of thousands of jobs by financial powers, against which the workers' struggle has proved powerless. The contradiction is present in this very space of the street, which is at once the classical site for the affirmation of a people and the last available space for community building. The two modalities of constituting a subjective force – being together against a world order that separates and sets people in competition, and fighting against the enemy – here maintain a distance from each other. This is to say that being together is unable to constitute itself as conflictual in its separation, in its very autonomy. Certainly in recent years, notably in Greece, we have seen forms of struggle and forms of collective affirmation return, some of which had seemed lost, but the forms of connection between self-affirmation and conflict that came out of it did not resolve the classic aporias of their relations.

ERIC HAZAN   If it is indeed true that work no longer creates a world (at least in the West), that we do not know what form to give to a 'new people', that we are deprived of any 'symbolic and lived world to lean on' – then is this an occasion for mourning or on the contrary an opportunity? Is the moment not about doing away with our inheritance of old ideas, our old forms of organization? Is it not about reflecting collectively on new ways of fighting, on novel forms of living?

JACQUES RANCIÈRE   New ways of fighting – this leads back to the question: what does it mean to fight? How is the *we* of the fight against the enemy constituted? Things would be simple, were the matter simply for actors of the same type to find good forms of struggle against the enemy. The problem touches on the very identity of the actors and on the question of what it means to act. An action is classically defined by the relationship between the deployment of an autonomous energy and the goal towards which this action tends. There was a time when the relation between the two came together in the equivocal expression 'take power', which said two things in one: that the deployment of an autonomous energy itself formed the very fabric of a new collective life (the 'republic of workers'), but also that specialized organs would seize specialized places and functions in order to exercise state power (the 'dictatorship of the proletariat'). Today no one knows what the seizure of power means; and the whole strategic vision, the very relationship between the means and the ends, has become an empty scholasticism. The question remains of the immanent future harboured by a given movement. But, to pose it, we must first pose anew the question of the time itself in which one situates it. The discovery is being made today that the history of equality is an autonomous history, that it is not the development of strategies built on an analysis of the objective transformations of technologies, of the economy, and so on but rather a constellation of moments – a few days, a few weeks, sometimes a few years – that creates its very own temporal dynamics, endowed with more or less intensity and duration. Each time a new beginning is created, and no one knows how far it will go. Moreover, the claim that lessons can be drawn from experiences does not actually lead very far. The idea of drawing lessons always presupposes that this time one will find the good way of doing what one wants to do. Unfortunately, it is not what one wants that determines the direction of a moment of equality. It is the other way around: the 'will' is a result – it is the modality that the deployment of the egalitarian moment takes. Rediscovering the monadic aspect of egalitarian moments also means rediscovering the ambiguity of these dynamics. Emancipation has always been a way of creating another time from within the normal order of time, a different way of inhabiting the sensible world in common. It has always been a way of living in the present in another world, as much as – if not more than – of preparing a world to come. One does not work for the future, one works to hollow out a gap, a furrow traced in the present, to intensify the experience of another way of being. This is what I've tried to say since *Proletarian Nights*. The armchair strategists were clearly not pleased. However, I do not see how or what to discuss if we do not start with the following: how are we to think through what is being willed when people come together, change the destination of a place and open a different time? How are we to rethink time and 'will' to speak about this?

ERIC HAZAN   You very correctly claim that the essential thing is to do away with the idea of domination as a great coherent system, and that domination operates, on the contrary, through a combination of heterogeneous elements and arrangements.

If we accept this idea, what about the widespread description of the 'current state of the world' as beset by a great black cloud – air pollution and terrorism, authoritarian drifts in Eastern Europe, massacres in the Middle East, the election of Trump, rise of the Front national in France . . . ? Ought we not to be suspicious of this globalizing view? Doesn't the matter rather concern a construction established by heterogenous and nevertheless convergent arrangements? In the question 'how did we come to be here?', who is this 'we' and where is this 'here'? In sum, ought we not to refuse this effect of globalization on thinking, to stop amalgamating different situations into a great defeatist mash?

JACQUES RANCIÈRE   In this matter, let's grasp the relationship to be thought through between four terms: the global and the differentiated, the mash and defeatism. And let's start with the last term: 'defeatism' is not 'the effect of globalization on thinking'. It is, quite simply, the effect of defeat, more precisely the effect of half a century of defeats of struggles and hopes. At the beginning of the 1960s, there was a feeling of a vast movement towards a freer and more equal world thanks to the emergence of the Third World, the Bandung Conference, the Cuban Revolution, the decolonization movements in Africa and the development of a secular and modernist nationalism in Arab and Muslim countries. At the end of these same years, the revolutionary movement saw a resurgence in the West and in Latin America. Then, at the end of the 1980s, much hope was born of the collapse of the Soviet empire. Lastly, there has recently been the formidable event of the Arab Spring. All these struggles were lost, all these hopes were dashed. Instead, we have had Thatcher's and Reagan's 'conservative revolution', the slow erosion of all social gains and the collapse of worker movements in the West, the various drifts of the former communist countries, dictatorships and corrupt governments in Africa and practically everywhere in the world, ethnic wars in former Yugoslavia, the rise of radical Islamism in the Middle East, and that of reactionary and racist forces throughout the West. Unless we adopt the puerile stance that consists in saying that all these defeats are excellent because they have swept away all the illusions and laid bare the naked reality of domination, we must set out from the following: the first problem today is not to try to go further ahead but to go against the flow of the dominant movement.

It is in relation to this balance sheet that the 'mash' offers its services: the mash, that is, the movement of totalization that relates all these defeats to one and the same first cause, sees in all the contemporary disasters one and the same catastrophe, and treats them as multiple forms of manifestation of a fundamental character, which defines the very type of world to which we belong. This metaphysical catastrophe goes by the name of acosmism, the domination of technology, the crisis of the symbolic and so on. These various formulations of the contemporary 'catastrophe' all have a common origin, namely the thought of Heidegger, expressed sometimes directly, sometimes via privileged intermediaries (Hannah Arendt, Levinas or Lacan), and sometimes even by taking in theorizations that stem from elsewhere, such as the situationist critique of the 'spectacle', which was originally sustained by Feuerbach and Marx but was quickly turned into a simple illustration of the great critique of the technicized world, in which the symbolic order has fallen into the swamp of the imaginary. All this might be cast aside by saying that such is the totalizing view of an outside spectator, but this would be to forget an essential point: namely that, more than the spectator, the actor is the one who needs a totalizing vision. And the great black cloud is not the sullen mood of the day; it is the form taken by the transformation of the specific type of totalization that sustained the struggles, hopes and possibly the triumphalism of bygone years.

This specific type of knotting is one that Marxism had established between two types of totality: one suited to action and one determined by science. Politics always has need of a certain globality: it needs a global division of the situation, a perception of the whole and a global affect. It is true that this globality, which carves out a scene, a situation, actors and actions, is very different from a global view of the world and from a global diagnostic. It rather proceeds via rarefaction. The characteristic of action in general is to reduce the factors of a situation, slicing into the infinite network of dependencies through which it is inscribed in a global reality in order to constitute the space of a subjectivation. The political assertion of some singular right, equality or solidarity does not busy itself with finding out whether the global order of a society or of a world is compatible with this assertion. In one sense the globality of action, which frames a scene and reduces the factors, is opposed to that of science, which links every particular phenomenon to the totality of a system of causes and effects. The problem is that, in the modern age, the emergence of the social sciences produced an underlying confusion between the two. Political action was claimed to depend on a science of history or society that set its conditions of possibility, actors, terrains and prospects for action. If there is a difference between the 'politics of the ancients' and the 'politics of the moderns', it does not lie in the reductive opposition between an ancient primacy of the collective and a modern primacy of the individual and of the liberties of what is individual. It lies in this modern demand – this metapolitical demand – that politics be deduced from a science of society and from the forces driving it. Of course, this demand is never actually satisfied. Science has the double draw-back of carving too broadly for action and losing itself in too many details that paralyse it. But, short of really guiding political action, Marxist science managed for a while to provide its spaces of subjectivation with temporal schemas, maps of the territory for action, forms of interpretation, a register of affects and of schemas that coordinate the interpretation of situations, the determination of actions and the sustaining of affects. It thus determined an equilibrium between both forms of globality. This equilibrium is what has been lost in this series of defeats, whereby not only were those in struggle and their hopes defeated, but so, too, were the very forms of articulation between perception, interpretation and action. There is no longer any knowledge of action that is legitimated by a science of society. The rigorous Marxist commentators who teach us every day on social networks to see the effect of the worldwide domination of capital in every situation have an answer for everything, but no longer does this 'answer for everything' forge any space of concordance between perception, thought, affect and action.

This is why post-Heideggerian thinking on the great catastrophe has more or less taken its place. The advantage of this thinking over Marxist science is that it defines a landscape and a global affect that enable the construction of a visibility and of a feeling of global horror, to which it is then possible to oppose a form of salvation posited as its absolute other. This salvation can be an umpteenth critique of humanism, anthropocentrism or Cartesianism that puts the defence of the earth, Gaia or the planet in the place of fighters for freedom and equality among humans. Or it can be the reassertion of communism as a pure, Platonic idea, unburdened by the Marxist science of history and by an analysis of global force relations carried out by some avant-garde. But this salvation can be thought of only against the backdrop of the great black cloud. There is, all the same, something that Badiou, Žižek or the Comité invisible [Invisible Committee] share with Finkielkraut, Houellebecq or Sloterdijk: it is this basic description of the nihilism of a contemporary world devoted to the servicing of goods and to the democratic enchantments of commodity narcissism. They view it from very different perspectives and draw entirely opposite conclusions from it. There is no question about that. It remains that this Heideggerian vision of a decadent world, calling for a radical turnaround, has taken the place of the Marxist vision of a revolution that liberates the potentialities that the forward march of the world has already formed.

But we cannot respond to this effect of the great cloud simply by saying that it is necessary to disentangle the elements of the situation and treat them separately. For the problem is to know how this differentiation is to be understood, who is the subject that effectuates it and in the name of which criteria. Differentiation does not mean escape merely from a 'great defeatist mash', but escape from the type of subjectivity whose latest product it is: the subjectivity that identifies the time of political action with the time of a global process and that, as a function thereof, determines the modes of articulation and hierarchization between elements. Now, this disentanglement exists in fact and gives rise to today's prevalent kind of militancy, the one that seizes upon a specific circumstance – a form of domination, a type of injustice – in a frame within which the elements of the situation are there, clearly definable, and within which it is known why, for whom and with whom one works. Such circumstances might include defending the rights of the poor people who are sent packing from their homes, or of the farmers who are driven from their land; fighting against a plan that threatens the ecological balance; welcoming those who have had to flee their country, preventing them from being sent back home and giving them the means to integrate right where they are; offering means of expression to those deprived of them; enabling this or that category of human beings disparaged for such and such a reason – sex, origin, physical ability, and so on – to impose a rule of equality; and thousands of other battles of this sort. What characterizes all these struggles is not simply their fixation on the particular, as is often said. What they challenge is the traditional schemas linking up the particular and the universal. The universality of a demand is asserted directly on each so-called partial terrain, without going through those forms of universalization that formerly integrated – or claimed to integrate – a particular target in a general battle. These battles may very well come together in demonstrations that hit back against global sorts of offensives (first employment contract and *loi Travail* in France, the demands of the troika in Greece . . .). Actors from such battles also assembled in squares in Madrid, Istanbul, New York and Athens, where, in the form of a movement, people gathered who had come from one or other specific form of mobilization – whether for the rights of women, the right to housing, ecology, alternative media, anti-racism and many other such causes. But this process of addition did not turn the movement into a collective that integrates partial struggles into a global battle. It is rather occupation itself, as an opposition between spaces and times, that constituted a shared being together: not by universalizing partial struggles, but by reasserting a global refusal of a global world that also cuts across all these struggles. In short, what happens in these large gatherings is the same thing that happens in the specific struggles. The singularization of struggles and the gathering together of actors occurs outside the idea of any fusion oriented by a view of history and the future. In some sense it is ways of creating the common and a common way of being that are being asserted in each circumstance – rather than a way of acting that would coordinate actions and synthesize their direction. Perhaps there is an ethical turn in politics here that is deeper and more radical than that which I analysed and denounced twenty years ago.

This also affects the question of the subject who might identify the *one* and the *there*. One would be hard-pressed today to identify the discourse of an active subjectivity, which synthesizes the experience of these different ways of constructing the common. Recent movements have given rise to much speech, but the very diversity of this speech has excluded that form of it which looks to grasp the global direction of the movement in an historical sequence. The *one* is, in a sense, the recognition that there is no *we* that bears within it the memory of everything that has happened to us since those times of great hope in the 1960s, no *we* that can assess all that, inscribe this assessment into the dynamic of recent struggles, and draw rules for action from it. What there is is singular assessments, letters to 'our friends', addresses to 'the youth'. There is, in particular, this constellation of individuals to which I belong: individuals who, on the basis of their experience of the past half-century, speak to youths who want to rediscover in this history reasons for hope that the actors of these experiences and experiments have often lost. There was a time when Badiou asserted that one could not speak about politics except as a militant, in other words from within an organization. Now he makes public interventions in which he claims to speak to no one but himself and addresses only listeners and readers at once actual and indeterminate. This remark does not imply any criticism, it simply underscores a factual shift. Today what we have is not the voice of a movement but singular instances of speech that attempt to think through the common power encapsulated in singular moments, maintain their actuality and keep open the space of their compossibility.

Eric Hazan   A slight shift in viewpoint. The singular manifestations of speech that you mention – even if they do not manage, or even seek, to endow the movement with a global meaning or to situate it in an historical sequence – do they not constitute an important movement? One can think that the aesthetic revolution that you have so well described, the one that which took place in the mid-nineteenth century and saw the emergence of critical modernity, is not without ties to the properly revolutionary movements of 1848

43

and their aftermath – a disaster somewhat comparable to what occurred after the hopes of the 1960s. If we accept this parallel, is it not logical to expect a new aesthetic revolution, repudiating both post-Heideggerian thought and the progressivist cultural hegemony? A new revolution, in the wake of the movement of the spring of 2016, with its fruitless assemblies and unprecedented and joyous demonstrations. Certainly, it will be difficult to re-tie the relation between culture and a politics that is so broken up, so devoid of any project – for we bear witness not to a distribution of the sensible, but to its fragmentation, which brings with it great wealth, but also considerable impotence.

What sort of cultural offensive could arise, then, that does not lay claim to hegemony – and it seems to me that we can glimpse the first signs of it here and there? Will literature once again be its terrain, or else cinema, or the digital universe, or the theatre?

JACQUES RANCIÈRE We must first agree on what we call an 'aesthetic revolution'. The process that I designated by this name is a very long-term process, two of whose essential aspects I have underlined: on the one hand, art became autonomous as a sphere of sensible experience, while abolishing the boundaries that separated the subjects and ways of doing that pertained in the Beaux Arts from the world of ordinary experience; on the other hand, the question that came to occupy the heart of revolutionary thought and practice was that of the transformation of sensible experience, and no longer only of institutions and laws. The aesthetic revolution, understood in this sense, establishes a link between phenomena whose global direction is shared but whose concrete forms, terrains of effectiveness, and results often remained separate. There is the introduction into the world of art of prosaic subjects, characters and situations, or so-called popular forms and the formal revolutions of the arts that resulted from it; but there is also the introduction, among common men and women, of forms of perception, sensibility and aspirations borrowed from so-called aristocratic culture. There is the constitution of an autonomous world of speech, forms and performances freed from their traditional social usages, but also the formation of new militant subjectivities and the establishment of programmes in which art is no longer

45

devoted to creating works but to transforming the frames of material life in all its aspects.

The fact that the social revolution conceived of by Marx was rooted in an aesthetic revolution appears clearly in the text – the only one somewhat developed – that he dedicated to the idea of communism, namely the third of the *Manuscripts of 1844*. Communism is defined in it as the humanization of the human senses. It is the state in which the exercise of the senses is, for everyone, its own end; there this exercise is no longer submitted to the crudeness of needs, itself the consequence of property. Beyond the immediate reference to Feuerbach, we see the extent to which this definition depends on the theoretical revolution formulated by Kant and Schiller. It is Kant who saw, in aesthetic judgement, a mode of apprehension of sensible experience in which in principle everyone participates, because it is indifferent to that which makes a sensible form a useful thing and a property belonging to an owner. It is Schiller who turned this affirmation of a shared human capacity into the principle of an equality conceived of in terms of sensible experience, and no longer in terms of institutions and laws. I have recalled many times that, by linking palpable liberty and equality to the abolition not only of the division of labour but of the very separation between the ends of an activity and its means, the 'human' revolution that the young Marx opposed to the political revolution reprised the core of the Schillerian idea of the aesthetic education of man. The revolution concerns the perceived and sensible world; it concerns everyday gestures and the manner in which beings relate to one another in it; it implies that these gestures and these relations have their end in themselves, and no longer in an external utility – such is the aesthetic heart of the Marxist idea of communism and revolution.

We know how this aesthetic principle continually came into conflict with the instrumental reason of the avant-gardes, the edification of 'bases' of socialism, of revolutionary discipline, and so on. We know how it was defeated in the Soviet revolution, along with this revolution itself, over the longer term. Since the defeat of Soviet artists from the revolutionary generation, one can say that the aesthetic revolution has become something like a great reserve of unaccomplished but always reactualizable possibilities. Let us think, for example, of the way in which surrealism gathered up in its words, its images and its fictions the heritage of the insurrectional city and passed it on to the new insurgent generation of the 1960s. Let us also recall how the new revolutionary sensibilities of these years contributed in turn to nourishing not only forms of art but also forms of sensibility and ways of creating community at a distance from official 'political' life.

Sociologists have sought to oppose a dubious artistic critique, always ready to be reconverted into a 'new spirit of capitalism', to good old social critique. But social critique itself was born on the terrain of the aesthetic revolution. It was born as a refusal of the dichotomy that assigns some, by fate, to the world of utility and others to the world of disinterested enjoyment. And, if the aesthetic forms of refusing the dominant order have come to acquire the importance that they have in recent decades, it is also because social critique, as they understand it, found itself orphaned, together with its avant-gardes, its programmes and its troops. By the same token, forms of political radicality have rediscovered their aspect of aesthetic distance from instrumental logics. Since mass demonstrations are no longer called by parties and unions but by innumerable micro-collectives instead, the great banners and watchwords of avant-gardes have given way to those multitudes of placards on which each person risks their own words – and possibly drawings, too. When occupation moved from the factory to the street, it had to dissociate its aspect related to the reconfiguration of common space and time from the form with which it had identified, namely the collective of workers taking control of the machinery of production. This explains the place that theatre people and performers have come to take, not as artists in the service of the people but as inventors of distancing gestures and dramaturgies. Since the development of journals and small publishing houses independent of all avant-gardist legitimacy, we have seen the assertion of a new solidarity between political radicality and an attention to words, gestures and images that is also an attention to typography and typesetting – it is a refusal to dissociate forms from contents or the outward appearance of words on a page from the propositions that they carry, or to separate the decidable meaning of an image from its undecidable affect. We know the polemics that arose recently around the exhibition

'Soulèvements' ['Uprisings'],[11] which was criti-
cized for having separated the forms of uprising
from their content. But the criticism bears no
weight if it aims simply to re-establish, against an
'aestheticizing' deviation, a hierarchy that asserts
the primacy of content over form. The criticism
holds only if it is taken in both directions and if
it is understood that the 'aesthetic' content of the
politics of emancipation is precisely the indissociation between the end and the means. In fact,
it is this principle of indifferentiation that today
produces a break from traditional forms of far-
left politics, that is, from their manner of putting
certain forms – electoral politics, protest action,
artistic production and so on – *at the service* of
more or less distant revolutionary ends. This
implies in fact a relation of proximity between
the radical political scene and the artistic scene,
providing each of them with new resources: on
the one hand, the new resources introduced into
political action through the inventions of per-

11 [Translator's note: The exhibition 'Soulèvements', curated
by Georges Didi-Huberman, took place at the Jeu de Paume
in Paris between 18 October 2016 and 15 January 2017. It was
a transdisciplinary exhibition that questioned the aesthetic and
political representation of peoples.]

formance, through linguistic discoveries, through the new embodiments of yesterday's words and fictions, but also through the mobilizing powers of the image circulated therewith; on the other, the gestures and images of this action, redisposed and rearranged in art venues that, besides, are known to rely on the very state institutions and financial powers against which this action fights.

If there is a specificity to our present, it lies in this mode of indecisive proximity between political militancy, attention to the transformations of forms of life, and a world of art marked more by the meeting of types of expression and the montage of their elements than by dynamics specific to already constituted art forms. I cannot hold out any belief in any kind of literature, theatre or cinema that would be, in itself, the expression of new sensibilities or a messenger of the future. What brings art closer to politics today is its interest in words and images, in movements, in times and in spaces, and in the diverse and shifting combinations of these elements (performance, *mise en scène*, installation, exhibition, etc.) rather than in an internal renewal of already constituted arts. Going further, one might say that one of the dominant characteristics of art today is that it establishes transversal links between ordinarily separate practices. Not only does the artist tend to become a sort of poly-technician assembling heterogeneous materials, technologies and modes of representation, he or she also engages, and often, in a specific work on common words, images, sounds or gestures that traverse the borders between artistic and prosaic activities. This search, by which the aesthetic revolution is pursued today, for a community between practices and worlds is something far more profound than the performances linked to the bureaucratic-style watchword that wants art to work towards mending the broken social bond. There is never any lack of a social bond. The whole question is to know which one. In art and politics alike, the common is given today as something to be constructed with heterogeneous forms and materials, and not as an act of affirming resources proper to constituted unities, be this a matter of social classes, specialized organizations or predefined arts. This form of proximity between the political and artistic processes that go towards composing the common entails confusions that often benefit art more than collective action; however, the critique of aestheticism itself, which claims to denounce these confusions, produces no political invention. The invention *hic et nunc* of forms of the common at a distance from the dominant forms remains, today, the crux of practices and ideas of emancipation. And emancipation, yesterday as today, is a way of living in the world of the enemy, in the ambiguous position of one who fights against the dominant order but is also capable of constructing within it separate places in which the common escapes its law.

ERIC HAZAN   One can agree – as I do – with the essentials of this reply, and in particular with the last sentence ('emancipation is a way of living in the world of the enemy . . .'). But one may wonder why we find so little spirit – not to say such a commonly shared depression – among those who devote time and energy to constructing the common in one or other of its forms. Hypothesis: if one accepts the capitalist rule of the game (market + profit), then all efforts end up hitting a wall. Even if a first barrier gets knocked down – a minister, a boss, a law, a court – behind it one finds a steel wall on which one reads: 'You see that it is indeed impossible.' Which is not fun. In these conditions, must we not lead the struggle on two fronts, which are so intertwined as to be indiscernible at times? On the one hand, wherever each of us finds him- or herself, to elaborate another 'way of inhabiting the sensible world in common'; and, on the other, despite the lack of model, despite the obsolescence of historical references, to act to change not the rules but the game itself – that is, to prepare an insurrection of a new type, one that aims neither at changing institutions nor at exercising power otherwise but at coalescing heterogeneous collective powers – powers based, among other things, on the movement that you describe in the domain of art – in order to break down the steel wall and clear out the rubble?

JACQUES RANCIÈRE   We agree on the fact that the construction *hic et nunc* of egalitarian forms of the common cannot be dissociated from struggle against the forms that structure the world of domination. Simply, there are several ways of thinking through this indissociation. And the notion of fighting on two fronts, with the hierarchy of tasks that it implies, is probably not the best way of formulating it. On this basis, in any case, two problems arise: that of the topography of domination and that of the meaning given to the word 'insurrection'.

Your question indeed suggests a certain topography: there are different enclosures against which one fights and may possibly win some partial victories, and there is the central fortress of capitalist power. This description does in fact lead to depression. And we know how a certain Marxism turned into the privileged propagator of this depression, as follows: nothing is of any use so long as we have not taken the impregnable fortress. This sort of theoretical stringency often goes along, in practice, with a rather bald opportunism as regards certain forms of strong-arm state power embodied in charismatic leaders, such as Hugo Chavez's 'twenty-first-century socialism'. We know how this vision of capitalist power entertains, moreover, a sort of resignation or complacency towards other forms of oppression – state, military, ethnic, sexual, religious or other – which come to be legitimated in fact as peripheral consequences of this central domination, leaving open the qualification of these same oppressive powers, according to the mood, either as simple agents of capitalist and colonial domination or as forms of resistance to it.

The image of the capitalist fortress is doubly misleading. On the one hand, it places economic exploitation in the role of a first cause on which other forms of oppression depend and would, by the same token, disappear upon the abolition of their cause. Yet this causal dependency has never been verified. That in our countries state powers have served and still serve capitalist interests does not entail any such causal hierarchy between forms of oppression. The two great anti-capitalist revolutions of the twentieth century were marked not by the withering of the oppressive powers of the state but, on the contrary, by their immoderate growth. And they led to another form of exploitation of living labour, since in fact the capitalist form is by no means the only form of economic exploitation. Current events show us, moreover, that diverse forms of oppression can be combined, opposed or substituted for one another. Let us think of the way in which the Tunisian and Egyptian revolutions against the state power's pillaging of the national wealth enjoyed the support of the army or of religious institutions prior to having these latter turn against them. It is clearly more convenient to say that all this is much of a muchness, that lurking behind everything is always the same power of global capital, which is able to manipulate and so on. It is well known that at night all cows are grey, but there are also people who fight to get out of the night.

On the other hand, the image of the great wall misleads by localizing enemy number one in its 'own' specific place, a central place that we must reach after first penetrating all the barriers, enclosures and mirages. But capitalist power is not something that remains hidden away behind the barriers of state power. First, state and economic powers are intertwined to a degree that they have never been before. Second and above all, capitalism is more than a power; it is a world, and it is the world in which we live. Today it is not the wall that the exploited must smash down to gain possession of the product of their labour. It is the air that we breathe and the web that connects us. It is the power that 'gives' work to Chinese, Cambodian and other proletarians to produce commodities at low prices, enabling wage earners, the unemployed and the semi-employed in the western world to maintain their living standards. It is the power that generates the profits able to be redistributed – through the intermediary of pension funds – as pensions to the common people in the United States or – through the intermediary of state finances – as RMI, RSA[12] or unemployment allowances on which, in France and other western countries, a number of enemies of capitalism live. We do not stand opposite capitalism but in its world, a world in which the centre is nowhere and everywhere, which does not mean that there is nothing to be done but that the figure of the 'head-to-head confrontation' never comes about as such. Even if material work and the direct extraction of surplus value play a far more important role in our western societies than is said, it is indeed difficult to imagine here today an anti-capitalist struggle as a head-to-head battle between the producers of surplus value and its seizers. The battle tends to dissolve itself into a more diffuse one, against the different forms according to which capitalist

12 [Translator's note: the *revenu minimum d'insertion* (RMI; minimum income) was a French form of social welfare. It targeted people without any income who were of working age but had no other rights to unemployment benefits. Created in 1988 under the socialist government of Michel Rocard, it was fully replaced on 1 June 2009 by the *revenu de solidarité active* (RSA; active solidarity income), a similar form of work welfare benefit officially aimed at reducing the barrier to return to work.]

logic demands our bodies and our thoughts, and transforms our environment and our lifestyles. This is why is it indeed difficult today to make a distinction between the supposedly central and objective struggle against the fortress of capital and emancipation from the modes of community that it constructs and the forms of subjectivity that it requires.

This is what makes it equally difficult to understand this new type of insurrection you talk about. Insurrection seems to be invoked above all as a substitute for the impossibility of grasping a central form of confrontation between the haves and the have-nots. But it is significant that, in your formulation, its novelty is characterized by its ends, that is, by the anticipation of what will happen after it, without any word being pronounced as to its very form. It seems nevertheless that the question of what we understand today by insurrection arises. In truth, it always does. If one takes the nineteenth century, the classical age of thinking about insurrection in France, we see that the word covers extremely different processes. Insurrection is, on a first meaning, the unforeseen uprising of human groups against such or such a form of injustice, an uprising that takes diverse forms, including street occupation, attacks on symbolic targets and erections of barricades that symbolize a secession of the people more than they could serve any war against those in power. It is, next, a clash that opposes the fractions of a politico-military force, which is that of the people in arms. June 1848 in Paris is not only a workers' insurrection; it also consists in the opposition of the popular fraction of the National Guard to its dominant bourgeoisie. The Paris Commune is the opposition of the popular National Guard to the power of Versailles and its army. On a third meaning, insurrection is the coup by which a professional revolutionary fraction attempts to seize the centres of state power. Between these three components, there has never been any stable synthesis. We know Blanqui's criticisms of the workers of June 1848, who gathered at random in the streets, were shut in their quarters and, through their barricades, closed themselves off from the possibility of acting as an organized army able to stage an offensive against central power. It remains that the insurrection of June 1848 actually took place, whereas the insurrection planned by the science of the professional revolutionaries Blanqui and Barbès in May 1839 simply did not, that it was merely an aborted coup, and that even Blanqui was unsure how to wrest control of the situation on that day in May 1848 when a popular demonstration invaded the National Assembly and named him member of an insurrectional revolutionary government.

Marxism came to overdetermine the already problematic unity of this politico-military form by identifying insurrection with the supreme moment of a historical process of class confrontation, and with the tipping point not only between one power and another but between one world and another. It is true that, in addition, the two world wars and the Japanese occupation of China masked the contradictions of the notion by giving to the second element of the insurrectional conjuncture – the split among the people in arms – the means to play the decisive role. The Bolshevik insurrection was the point not of departure but of arrival of a revolutionary process born of the conjunction between a working-class protest movement and a revolt from some of the troops that tsarist power had armed for foreign warfare before the provisional government armed the workers for their own defence. Simply, the storming of the Winter

Palace was still far from being the destruction of capitalism, which itself was not the end of the oppression. As for the victory of the Chinese revolution, it was, properly speaking, the victory of one army against another. It is pointless to hold forth on what became of each of these experiences. One thing is certain: those who talk today about insurrection in fact give up on the real history of insurrectional processes and feign to ignore that the people in arms no longer has any reality in our societies. The reference to insurrection in 'radical' discourse means two things only. First, it emblematizes a global refusal of the existing order. It asserts that the reigning system must be destroyed. But it does not thereby define any specific form of action. Second, it asserts the necessity of violence. But more than violence is required for an insurrection to occur and in some sense to rattle the power of capital. The paradigm by which some are fascinated, that of the riots in the banlieues in 2005, typically obeys a model of protest that goes after symbolic targets and defends its territory against the forces of order without any anti-systemic aims. And destroying shop windows and ATMs in order to 'radicalize' protests deemed too well-behaved is no more insurrectional than the peaceful assemblies of Nuit debout.

Significantly, when the book titled *The Coming Insurrection* tackles, *in extremis*, insurrection itself, it does so in order to take a distance from all forms of planned activism. After having posited that the decision must 'take us' rather than us taking it, it gives insurrection the task of 'running the police around' rather than 'being run around by them', so that by 'forcing them to be everywhere, they can no longer be effective anywhere', and asks revolutionaries to take up arms so that they do not have to use arms.[13] Some years later, its authors believe to have observed that these insurrections did indeed occur, but without bringing about what they had expected; not only were these insurrections not the 'revolution' but, further, they signed the death warrant of revolution as a process. In this logic, what was in fact most 'insurrectional' in the squares movements was what they did out of necessity to organize everyday life, showing, in short, that insurrection is in fact the self-organization of life by ordinary

13 Comité Invisible, *The Coming Insurrection*, Los Angeles, CA: Semiotext(e), 2009: 120–8 (translation modified).

people, who stand against the chaos character-
izing the organization of life from above.[14] To
prepare the insurrection means, then, no longer
to prepare it, no longer to want it, but simply
to watch, according to the same authors, for the
'patient growth of its power'. In sum, we come
back to the idea that the only way to prepare
the future is not to anticipate it, not to plan it,
but to consolidate, for themselves, forms of subjective dissidence and forms of organization of
life at a distance from the prevailing world. We
come back to the idea, which I have long held,
that presents alone create futures and that what is
vital today is to develop forms of secession from
the modes of perception, thought, life and community proposed by inegalitarian logics. What is
vital is the effort to enable these forms to come
together and produce the accrued power of a
world of equality. In these conditions, the word
'insurrection' has a chiefly emblematic value –
unless it is a way of taking back with the left hand
what one has feigned to give up with the right
hand, namely the idea of 'taking power' as the

14 Comité Invisible, *To Our Friends*, trans. Robert Hurley,
Los Angeles, CA: Semiotext(e), 2015: 231–3.

occupation of the machine's central organ by a unitary force.

ERIC HAZAN This reply contains many points with which I am in agreement, but not to the extent of going along with the conclusions you draw from them. First of all, capitalism, you say, is the world in which we live – a world in which the centre is everywhere and nowhere. Does this definition, which rings rather true, not risk leading to a renunciation, to a sort of secular quietism? If capitalism is the air we breathe, does it not, nonetheless, have a materiality whose brutality intensifies by the day, something easy to observe from the media to hard discounters, from refugees to the suburban transport lines? If it has no centralized commandment, does it not have strategies? In short, ought we to remain content with a diffuse battle against the forms of subjectivity induced by capitalism? Ought we not to define our own strategies? – Podemos or *cortège de tête*, dual power or the long march through the institutions?

Next, insurrection. Those who talk about it today, you say, give up on real history and do not define any specific form of action. Alongside your correct and interesting elaboration on June 1848, on Blanqui and on October 1917, no mention is made of the fundamental insurrection in the summer of 1789. Is this not a way – assuredly implicit – of accepting the *negationism* that impacts the French Revolution, of accepting the commemorative hijacking of this popular insurrection, which, despite Thermidor, Bonaparte and the Holy Alliance (among other things), nevertheless changed the world? Despite the past, ought we not to keep this insurrection in mind, an insurrection that no one saw coming or even prepared, and whose victorious dynamic took hold although no one knew where it would lead? In other words, can we dismiss the idea of insurrection by arguing that today it lacks an agent – the people – and a clear definition, with a model and a programme?

JACQUES RANCIÈRE   I will reply by starting with the last point. The argument about the French Revolution seems to me doubly shaky. If it is intended to prove that an insurrection may always occur without anyone having prepared or foreseen it, it is irrefutable. But the only logical conclusion to be drawn from this is that it is pointless to concern oneself with predicting or preparing one. If the point is intended to present the French Revolution as an event arising from a popular insurrection that erupted all of a sudden in a peaceful, serene sky on 14 July 1789, it is clearly wrong. The sky was by no means calm in July 1789. Had it been, the storming of the Bastille would have been just another 'popular emotion', one more violent than others but of the same type. If it was different, it is because there was the Assemblée in Versailles and its challenge to royal power; and it is because preparations for the Estates General and the conflict of Versailles had set the scene for the coming into existence of the nation as a collective reality and of the people as a political subject. For there to be a popular insurrection, there must be a people, which means a political subject. Here again, the habit – lazily Marxist – of opposing the reality of mass movements to parliamentary life conceived of as simple 'appearance' produces disastrous results. The French Revolution loses its meaning and its value as a model for the future if we forget the enormous political, juridical and ideological work that constituted the very scene in which the word 'revolution' took on a new meaning, in which

an insurrection is distinguished from an emotion
or from a riot, and in which the people exists as
subject. What properly characterizes this revolution is its extraordinary invention of institutions
– official or parallel – and of symbols; it is its
work of re-elaboration of the perceptible and of
the thinkable. This is the political imagination
that changed the world. This imagination is what
is cruelly lacking today; and it is not offset by the
call that some make for communes and others for
the resurrecting of the party and of the soviets.

Secondly, air: I do not know of anything more
material in the life of humans than air. On condition, of course, that it is not understood as it was
in my youth, namely as a metaphor of the 'ideol-
ogy' in which one spontaneously 'bathes'. What
I meant was the following: capitalism is not a
fortress that we find ourselves facing. It is not
simply a force that we endure; it is an environment in which we live, a milieu that determines
the normal type of things with which we have to
deal, the acts and behaviours through which we
relate to them, the relations into which we enter
with one another. There was a time when the
belief predominated that these types of relations
to things and to others, produced by domination,

were themselves beneficial to the battle and to the new world to come. It was the era in which it is was thought that the discipline of the capitalist factory would shape that of the combatants who destroyed the old world and that of the builders of the new one. The history of the Soviet Union and of the communist parties of the twentieth century showed that this was not the logical outcome. Moreover, the forms of capitalist discipline themselves diversified. When it comes to the authors of the *New Spirit of Capitalism*, some found in this an occasion to bemoan the loss of the values of solidary and disciplined group to the benefit of the 'artistic' – or 'petit bourgeois', as one said back then – values of autonomy and creativity. Others concluded, conversely, that, with immaterial production, capital now directly forms the practice and mode of subjectivity of communist cooperation. Both arguments, I believe, are misleading. Capital has not taken possession of our neurons. Nor has it formed the collective intellect of communism. But it is the milieu in which we live and act and in which our activity normally reproduces the conditions of domination. In this enveloping milieu one attempts to dig holes, to fit them out and to enlarge them rather than to marshal armies for battle. These holes, or openings, are very diverse in nature. They include organizations of struggle and battles against enemy offensives, all occurring within the diverse forms mentioned here; symbolically occupied sites that call for moments of fraternity, but also attempt to engage in the collective organization of material life; informal friendships and networks of circulation of thought, but also production cooperatives; attempts at forming community; diverse forms of mutual help; modes of circulation of information, and knowledges that, in various ways, allow one to live within a world organized by domination such that one escapes its rules of use . . . In all these forms of distance, what is henceforth foregrounded is the impossibility of separating the means of the struggle from its ends, the ways of being and acting together in the present from their distant objectives. This effectively constrains us to rethink the notion of strategy. To date, it has been dominated by two models: the model of adapting – or subordinating – means to ends; and the model of alliance, of the aggregation of forces, possibly updated through Ernesto Laclau and Chantal Mouffe's notion of 'chains of equivalences'. Despite everything, this always amounts to adding together constituted identities. Recent movements seem to me to urge us to understand the notion of strategy differently. In these movements, strategy becomes the specific power of expansion of a movement or a form; the capacity to link not one organization to another but a form of action, a type of gathering, one terrain of action to another. This is the sense in which I said above that the right outcome for Nuit debout might have been a rarely seen intervention into the domain of institutions, for example a campaign for the non-presidency. This means getting outside the following dilemma: either one remains uselessly faithful to the 'horizontal' purity of an occupation movement or one enlists in a party of 'left of the left' for reasons of effectiveness. We know that this is how the problem presented itself for some activists in Greece and in Spain, activists who thought it better to support Syriza or Podemos than to get stranded in a movementist democracy. Simply put, the problem immediately presents itself again: what sort of effectiveness is one talking about? For whom is it essentially effective that an increased percentage of voters is represented in an election: the dynamic of the movement or the solidity of the system of which this election is part? There is no response that is inevitably determined in advance: many 'purists' have become lost and, conversely, there are pragmatists who have stayed the course. The question is not to know whether one must be realistic or intransigent. It is to know the type of people with which one identifies: the people constructed by the dominant system or the egalitarian people under construction. Now, there is a section of the left today calling for a 'left populism' in which is adopted the very figure of the people that the system produces as its other: that of the people scorned by the elites, substantial and suffering, a figure that finds expression in a force that represents it authentically and in a leader who embodies it. This form of antagonism remains confined to being a balancing act between representation and embodiment, which is ultimately a balancing act between two forms of inegalitarian logic. Yet the problem is to oppose not groups, but worlds: a world of equality and a world of inequality. If there is a logic of distancing from the world organized by financial and state powers, it must be able, whatever paths it crosses, to have its own modes of action, instruments of action and agendas, which should be independent of those of the established order, even if it is brought to interact with them. This effectively implies that a certain unitary force comes to constitute itself on the basis of the so-called movementist logic that prevails today; on the basis of it, but not against it. And, above all, not by neglecting to ask the question: what is this 'we' that wonders whether 'we ought not our-selves to define some strategies'? This 'we' does not exist like the constituted centre from which one might ask 'What is to be done?' or 'How should we proceed?'. It exists only as a subject of discourse and as a way of speaking. Such is merely one of these multiple holes piercing the dominant order of which I spoke: a fictional hypothesis that can take on meaning only by being tied to other hypotheses, other propositions of world that go towards making so many various holes in the fabric of the dominant world.

ERIC HAZAN Some years ago you wrote: 'The greatest misfortune of a thought, is when noth-ing resists it.' In your way of understanding and explaining the world in which we are plunged, what resists, Jacques Rancière?

JACQUES RANCIÈRE I said that concerning machineries of thought such as that of Jean Baudrillard in which the Gulf War, the fall of the Twin Towers or the catastrophe of the Heysel Stadium all dissolve into virtual reality. Resistance is that which troubles thought, but also that which benefits it by resisting it. That said, there are many sorts of resistance. There is the resistance of objections, which, in my case, does not play a major role, since the majority of those who criticize me confine themselves to bemoaning that I talk about what I do and do not talk about what I do not do. This is neither very troubling nor very useful. Next there is the resistance of the object one talks about. This resistance is, in my case, massive and beneficial. What ought to be thought about the objects that have continually occupied me, about the texts that I've read a hundred times over, about the works that have accompanied my life, what one can say about them and in what way one can do so – for me these are things that must be worked on again and again. In this sense, I do not risk partaking in the misfortune of those who have one method for assimilating everything. Indeed, for me the method for talking about an object must always be drawn from this object itself, which is not preconstituted but is actually defined in this work, moves with the way in which one approaches it, in which one seeks to name it, describe it, conceptualize it. Thus the notions at stake in our conversation – people, politics, revolution, history and others – do not, for me, have any general definition on the basis of which I would judge given situations. On the contrary, situations present circumstances on the basis of which the meaning and possible scope of these words can be grasped. What is meant by 'people' or 'democracy' in the practice of our governments today, in the practice of those who demonstrate in the streets and set up their tents in squares, of those who deal with these words in their discourse? What is meant by 'art' in the case of such and such a type of image, performance or exhibition? The 'resistance' of the object is consubstantial with the work itself. This also means that each sentence that I write, each analysis that I propose is, for me, always problematic; it means that I formulate it always with the feeling that perhaps this is not it, that this might be false. From this angle I can say: everything resists me, and it's a good thing.

Now, there is a third form of resistance, which is absent in my case: the resistance of the milieu in which these words are proffered. Such is, for example, the resistance that the political activist encounters in relation to an idea that does not 'work', to a line that does not attract the assent of those for whom it was intended, to a solution that does not resolve the problem posed. From this viewpoint, I can say that my words do not encounter any resistance. These are the words of an individual who attempts to explain the world in which he lives without claiming to give determinate individuals or groups methods of action to verify. This is the Jacotot method once more: 'I must teach you that I have nothing to teach you', to which I add, for my audience, that it is up to them to know what they want and, as a consequence, the meaning that my words can take on for them. There are people whom these words displease. This is why they avoid reading me or listening to me. And there are people whom these words please, for example members of audiences who regularly tell me that these words give them hope, even if I don't have the feeling of having opened any particular future perspective. What gives them hope, at bottom, are words that are produced outside those logics that say what should be done and explain that, because it is not being done and indeed cannot be done, everything is going badly.

The status of this non-resistance is itself ambiguous. It can be said to be synonymous with irresponsibility. This is the judgement of realists, whether they are opportunistic socialist politicians or the intransigent collaborators of diehard Marxist magazines. But it can be said that this 'irresponsibility' signifies something more profound: an upheaval in the very system of address. It characterizes a 'reality' in which speech has lost its guarantees – and, above all, the guarantee that the subject of which it spoke and the one to which one spoke was one and the same and was itself legitimated by this homonymy. Not so long ago, we knew times in which the same 'proletariat' existed in texts and in reality. However forcibly Althusser denounced the confusion between real object and object of thought, Althusser spoke *about* the workers movement *to* the workers movement and did so *from within* the workers movement. Even by commenting on the *1844 Manuscripts* in one's room, one was included in this circle, and whoever was not part of this was said to be 'talking in the desert'. That this distribution of spaces is no longer ours is something that Bernard Aspe has clearly high-lighted at the beginning of *L'Instant d'après*, by evoking the importance taken on lately by 'oases'.[15] Freely taking up this term, I would say that a discourse on the present that gives hope to people who gather together to listen to a phil-osopher is a small oasis. An occupied city square, a ZAD[16] – these are oases of an entirely other dimension, certainly, but perhaps not differ-ent in nature: spaces of freedom 'in the middle' of the desert, except that the 'desert' is not the void but the overflow of consensus. And con-sensus is precisely the predetermined agreement between subjects, places, modes of enunciation

15 Bernard Aspe, *L'Instant d'après: Projectiles pour une poli-tique à l'état naissant*, La Fabrique, 2006 : 7–23.

16 [Translator's note: To begin with, the French acronym ZAD officially designated a *zone d'aménagement différé* (zone for future development). As groups have come together to defend the people and values of these zones, many of these development plans, such as the high-profile one in Notre-Dame-des-Landes, have been subject to challenge and occupation. Inverting its sense, a ZAD has thus come to be known as a *zone à défendre* (zone to defend), which is to say an area subject to a militant occupation that is intended physically to blockade a develop-ment project.]

and forms of efficacity. Today we are perhaps in the following ambiguous situation: on the one hand, the speech of people like me is deprived of the resistance that would provide it with a mode of articulation of the old theory–practice type. On the other, it has what power it can have from the very fact of standing outside any predetermined articulation with a type of action, a form of organization, a channel of diffusion, and so on, in order to address itself solely to a 'free' gathering of readers or listeners. This reconnects with what I said about modes of address to 'our friends' or to 'the youth'. Speech that today keeps open the possibility of another world is the kind that ceases to lie about its legitimacy and its effectiveness and assumes its simple status as speech – an oasis alongside others, or a separate island among other islands. Between these islands there is always the possibility of tracing links. This is at least the bet proper to the thinking of intellectual emancipation. And it is the belief that authorizes me to attempt to say something about the present.

POLITY END USER LICENSE AGREEMENT

Go to http://politybooks.com/eula/ to access Polity's ebook EULA.